Soldier Stories
Prisoner of War

Cornelius P. Thomas Jr.

© 2025 by Cornelius Thomas Jr.
Lyrical Giant Media Group

All rights reserved, including the right to reproduce this book or portions thereof in any form whatsoever by author. No part of this book may be reproduced, scanned, or distributed in any print or electronic form without permission. Please do not participate or encourage piracy of copyrighted materials in violation of author's rights.

Library of Congress Cataloging – in Publication Data

Thomas, Jr. Cornelius P.
(Poems, Text)
Sign of the Times
ISBN 978-0692969229

*This book was birthed out of the construction process
dedicated to soldiers in every walk of "life"
Since my steps were already ordered
the testimonies and documents recorded are precise
(Psalms 37:23-24)*

FOREWORD

Each and every day, we race in and out of each other's lives in a uniformed fashion. We, the people, have become so submerged and self-absorbed in our own personal issues. We hardly ever take time to consider the struggles that our neighbors may be enduring. So many people are screaming silently in an attempt to rid themselves of unfavorable circumstances, dilemmas, and temporary frustration. Due to the fact that none of us are exempt from trials, tribulations, and mortality, God has given humanity rules, guidelines, and standards to live by. In the midst of uncertain times, people in every walk of life are at war with something.

In *Soldier Stories: Prisoner of War,* Cornelius P. Thomas Jr. poetically takes the reader on a journey in which he exposes tactics of an unseen enemy, provides Godly wisdom, and instruction. He speaks truth in its rarest, yet, rawest form. God has given His vessel revelation knowledge based upon sound doctrine from the Word of Life. This book is very informative for those who seek a greater understanding of the spiritual war. In all actuality, this war is the root cause contributing to the conflicts that we face in life. People are destroyed for the lack of knowledge.(Hosea 4:6 KJV) However, it isn't God's will that anyone should perish and fall short of His promise of restoration through the Savior, Jesus Christ. This book provides clarity that can pave the way to transformation and freedom. As you take in the words of truth that leap off of the pages, allow God to dissect the heart, bring divine order, and reveal Kingdom principles. The Holy Spirit is giving insight to the Body, reaching out to the lost, downtrodden, and brokenhearted, as He reveals Christ all throughout the text. I don't take this opportunity to be a part of the poetic revolution for granted. God has placed an amazing work in the hands and heart of the author. I know that lives will be blessed.

Minister Kenya Harris

TABLE OF CONTENTS

Foreword

BASIC TRAINING IN THE VALLEY

Prisoner of War 2

Discipline 4

Individuality 6

Soldier Stories 8

Take a Stand 11

Key Instruments of War 14

Not My Will 16

The Fallen Soldiers 18

Battle Cries to the Believer 20

Missing Piece to the Puzzle 22

End Time Warriors 25

End Time Warriors *Extended* 28

Through it All, There is Hope II 31

Reporting Live From The Scene 34

Playing for Keeps 37

City Under Siege 39

Light Afflictions 41

TRANSFORMING THROUGH THE TRANSITION

Can't Be All Things 44

Lift Up A Standard 46

With Hopes To Deliver 48

Bold Expression 50

Crossing Over 52

A Heavenly Perception 54

The Emergency Alert System 57

The Struggle Continues 60

That I May Know Him 62

Ballads Of A Foreign Soldier 64

Conditioning 66

The Set-Up 68

The Verbal Assassin 70

Cries Of Anguish 72

The Gateway 75

Prisoner Of War II 77

The Potter's Wheel 79

FROM THE PROCESS TO THE PROMISE

Soldier Stories II 82

The Strategy I 84

The Strategy II 86

The Strategy III 88

The Strategy IV 90

The Strategy V 94

In All Thy Ways 97

Warfare in the Heat of the Day 99

By The Hand Of YAH 102

One Life At A Time 105

Nothing Is Impossible For God 107

Bless The LORD At All Times 109

The Sniper 111

Effective Immediately 113

The Execution Of Marching Orders 116

Amen 118

BASIC TRAINING IN THE VALLEY

PRISONER OF WAR
2 Chronicles 20:15, 2 Corinthians 10:3-5

If they're gone, then they left for a reason
and I'm good with that
That means the connection was for a season
wisdom dictates how I should react
I can discern the rats
flee from snakes revealed as fakes
Motives inspired by hate
destruction is the world's fate

Still called to walk in love
those redeemed can't afford to get super spiritual
Good hearts get drug through the mud
however I'm still expecting miracles
as a prisoner of war
Equipped with grace to go the distance
battle scars ignite poetry bars
From a warrior enlisted
in this supernatural army
These demons cannot harm me
lamentations exposed as the sun sets
Joy comes in the morning

Draped in the *Armor of ELOHIYM*
sprayed on the garment of praise
Complemented by prophetic apparel
spoken by the *Creator of Days*
I've been hidden for several seasons
overlooked and despised

Cornelius P. Thomas Jr.

Consumed by Holy Ghost fire
to sound the trumpet as a war cry
A prisoner of YAH who's aware
that warfare is always present
Battles in the mind, warring in your body
a decision to be slothful or pick up your *Weapon*

I plead the *Blood* against principalities, powers,
and rulers of darkness sent to hinder destinations
The oppressors continue to bog down the nations
spiritual wickedness in high places
ELOHIYM isn't bound by political systems
therefore we go against the grain
Knowing that all power is in Jesus' name
we expect the prophetic rain
To drop down on the nations
we await a worldwide revival
There's a great awakening in place for them
who are in the mode of survival

Faith determines survival
just like endurance wins the race
Through dreadful seasons and strenuous testing
the *Potter's Wheel* keeps us in shape
We keep a perfect praise on our lips
because the threat of circumstances can smother you
I stand only because I can
as a *P.O.W.*

DISCIPLINE
Matthew 16:24

Discipline is required
for soldiers who represent the *Messiah*
We grow by process
in life, we're tried by the fire
All of humanity is searching for something
as inhabitants of the earth
The *ELOHIYM of all flesh* is the only One
who can truly reveal your worth
There is a dream and there's reality
in between those two landmarks, we need dedication
Seasons come and go according to schedule
have to stay committed to reach the desired destination
The sacrifices that are made today
will pay off on tomorrow
Does your daily activity take you towards rejoicing or sorrow?

Circumstances will arise that induce stress
I suggest that you stand in defiance
There's always a bigger picture present
like small things to a Giant

Before honor we embrace humility
promotion comes from the Lord
In a weary land, He's my stability
He can heal those wounded and scarred
The process begins after initiation
accepting Christ through salvation

Cornelius P. Thomas Jr.

Basic training in the valley
discipline is developed through patience

If any man desires to follow Christ, he must first deny
himself and pick up his cross
We're living in a time where everyone wants to be seen
and heard, this is why multitudes are lost

SOLDIER STORIES: P.O.W.

INDIVIDUALITY
Psalms 139:14

Someone else's opinion of you doesn't have to be
accepted as your reality
We all have individual roles to play
we were created different, victims of mortality
Liken these times to the *Dark Age*
although the Spirit is speaking and the *Light* is shining
In this *Book of Life*, we turn the page daily to stay on
schedule with temporary assignments

The King's kids are being conditioned to inherit the
modern day *Promised Land*
Talents and purposes go hand in hand
once we seek YAH'S plan
Some think that life is overrated
time is our most valuable asset
It is appointed once for a man to die
this game of life, you can fail or pass it

There is a time to live
there is a time to die
We reap what we sow in a cycle
a time to laugh and cry
Those who are the closest to you
can be persuaded to become your foes
Because, evil lurks in secret
the hatred tends to grow
Everyone has fallen short of YAH's glory
Who among men can deny it?

Cornelius P. Thomas Jr.

He's all-seeing and all-knowing
nothing is hidden or private
One day, we all have to face the *Uncompromised Truth*
my number was called, but I put up a fight
It was hard for me to kick against the pricks
although I was bound by the evils of the night life
At least it seemed that way
all along *The Most High* had a purpose
At the end of the day, I had to keep it real with myself
without YAH'S favor, I would never surface
or rise to my full potential
I realized my dire need
was to get to know my *Creator*
Direction is better than speed
Many of my peers bumped their heads
the brick wall is tied to the destructive path
Everyone has been blessed with the freedom of choice
I have to stay faithful to my task
They mocked my radical behavior
tried to bring me to an open shame
Learned to live without the approval of men
I trust in the *Name that is above all names*
Why should I follow the pattern of the crowd when none
of them are truly succeeding?
Taking two steps forward and four steps backwards
reckless driving and speeding
Overlooking the traffic signs of life
more wisdom and knowledge is what I desire
Life is for learning not to be limited
Had to take heed before time expired

SOLDIER STORIES
2 Timothy 2:1-4

Words of pain that inspire change
the Christ was mocked, beaten, and put to shame
The servant is not greater than his *Master*
we grow by process, as we're trained
Called to go against the grain
in a time where information is running rampant
It all started with the tree of knowledge of good and evil
now, a generation of vipers are causing damage
He that dwells in the *secret place of The Most High*
can see through the "Eyes of Eternity"
and watch as time goes by

ELOHIYM has a purpose
can't run and hide from the "ugly truth"
"Dressed up" lies are embraced
have to judge the tree by its fruit
Can't continue to trim branches and not pluck the root
expecting different results to manifest
I became immortal when I gave in to *Time's Creator*
called out of dysfunction to withstand the tests

Pulled out of the dirt, muck, and mire
to join the winning team of *Kingdom Builders*
Delivered from a traumatized mental state and hopeless
conditions to become a *Giant Killer*
With recorded testimonies that can bless billions
dwelling among self-professed savages and villains
Animalistic conditioning suggested by the serpent

Cornelius P. Thomas Jr.

murder has replaced morals among lost children

The *Church* suffers persecution
while false leaders make vain contributions
Residents are trapped in warzones
filled with darkness and pollution

I've viewed the victims of countless murder scenes
they wanted to murder me
Before I came to the knowledge, Jesus was my *Shield*
now assigned adversaries assassinate me verbally
Coming from a suffocated section
where we grew up addicted to the fast life
In a rush to go nowhere
How can we get the cash right?
...the worth is in the dash right?
Only if they grasp Christ
The harvest is plentiful, the laborers are few
the fruit is perishing, past ripe

Tests, trials, and tribulations
condition soldiers to stand strong
In the past, we paid no attention to the truth
we were too busy doing wrong
The drama started to hit home
one day you're here, the next you're gone
The extermination among the youth
and the list goes on

Apprehended to dry out, YAH provided the hideout
grew sick and tired of hopeless conditions

SOLDIER STORIES: P.O.W.

to the Living God I cried out
He said, *"Now you'll take My route, deliver your
brothers and sisters that are held captive.
Everyone won't receive My Word
however, you cannot be passive."*

Took the heavenly oath and entered basic training
separated from making excuses and complaining
With enemies on every hand
ELOHIYM began priority rearranging
Delivered from the street life
for a purpose with a greater cause
A soldier in the trenches, it's not about me
forsaking pride, vainglory, and applause
They won't believe you until you make it
praying to discern the real from the fake
what's profane and what is sacred
Documenting soldier stories
allowing the *Spirit of Truth* to go before me
My life is hidden in Christ
we must give YAH the glory

Cornelius P. Thomas Jr.

TAKE A STAND
Joshua 1:9

If you don't stand for something
you will fall for anything
Because evil lurks in secret
we have to check for plots and schemes
The physical form is for a moment
eternity is in the unseen
Trusting in the *Prince of Peace*
He was manifested to redeem

In my flesh, there's a thorn
observing movements undercover
Jesus came to warn
He will stick closer than a brother
I'm sounding the alarm
to warn friends, enemies, or lovers
Our families have been destroyed and torn
because we don't confess true feelings to one another
So many faults and imperfections
stumbling blocks are in the way
We have a *Higher Power*
He can hear us when we pray
Whether one is lost or saved
sin will cause men to go astray
Sound doctrine reveals Christ
His grace has sustained me this day

You can identify a person by the fruit of their tree
The death, burial, and resurrection was for us to

SOLDIER STORIES: P.O.W.

be free
The way to walk is by faith
disregard what you see
Deliverance is my plea
I shout the victory, because it belongs to me

When you seek the *Kingdom of ELOHIYM*
then your life becomes hidden
A bad apple can spoil the bunch
meaning some fruit is forbidden
Learning to follow the *Spirit*, then lead
will yield good fruit on the mission
Jesus has set the captives free
but countless minds are in prison
We were redeemed to overcome
because the *Savior* has risen
He has given gifts to men
promotions and heavenly positions
As there's a time to receive
there's a time for giving
Every breathing soul has a purpose
a reason for living

The knowledge and power of YAH
the carnal minds can't comprehend it
He gives comfort to those who mourn
broken hearts, He can mend them
He's a *Purifier* and *Sanctifier*
The *Word* isn't bound, He's Transcendent
This same *Word* can save, heal, or deliver
the principles will be embraced by a remnant

Cornelius P. Thomas Jr.

Greater is *He* who dwells within me
than he who wreaks havoc in the land
The Holy Spirit is my *Leader, Guide*, and *Teacher*
He gives me clarity to understand
I find my rest and refuge in ELOHIYM'S
unchanging hands
I no longer fall for anything
because I was called to *take a stand!*

SOLDIER STORIES: P.O.W.

KEY INSTRUMENTS OF WAR
Ephesians 6:10-18

Today, I am in a state of seclusion
stuck in my own zone
Have to build according to plan
as the weak declares that they're strong
Learning how to be committed and carry my cross
without complaining
In this spiritual war
I AM a soldier in training
I've had to endure countless storms
blessed to be alive, I'm thankful
Had to leave the past behind
it was somewhat painful
We war within ourselves
What's the motive behind the attacks?
The devil wants us stranded
blinded by sin on our backs
The Savior is like a driver who picks up hitchhikers
On the journey, He will clean you up
patch up your wounds as a *Battle Fighter*
The *Tear Wiper* has already won the war
life is just a repeat of the same
We experience heartaches and hardships
to find that power is in Jesus' name
The Alpha and Omega
I offer Him praise, glory, and honor
There's only one way to survive during warfare
we have to keep on the whole armor

Cornelius P. Thomas Jr.

Harmless as doves, wise as serpents
we have to keep moving from level to level
We have power to stand against
and overcome the wiles of the devil
It is through revelation knowledge of the *Word*
that I can find out who I AM
My loins draped with truth
which reveals *The Unspotted Lamb*
He has brought me through the fire
He will take me through the flood
A bigger picture is present
the war is not against flesh and blood
A man chases his destiny
then comes his death date
We can stand if we wear righteousness
as a breastplate
False prophets cause people to error
setting the stage for the mark of the beast
Our feet has to be prepared with the *Gospel of Peace*
These days are filled with evil
corrupted minds are explicit
Only the shield of faith
can block the fiery darts of the wicked
We pray and confess better days
solidified as a holy nation
In order to keep a renewed mind
we need the helmet of salvation
The Word of God, a supernatural sword
we stand against all odds
God can heal our battle scars
these are the *key instruments of war*

SOLDIER STORIES: P.O.W.

NOT MY WILL
Luke 22:42

I'm up before the sunrise
with a military mind frame
Early will I seek YAH
with faith to go against the grain
Been tried by the fire
therefore my eyes possess a glare
Filled with passion and determination
spectators only see a blank stare
Delivered from street wars to enlist in the real war
now I represent the *Eternal Savior*
He allowed me to shake the inferiority-complex
He replaced it with His uncommon favor
I know that He is the *"Real Deal"*
against all odds, I'll give Him the glory
Reporting live from the combat zone
introducing the masses to *Soldier Stories*
Some struggle just to get through each month
fear overthrows effort and causes time to be wasted
We all need the *"Spiritual Immune Builder"*
many minds are heavily sedated
I was once bound by depression from the issues within
toxic associates despise
My very existence
smiling in my face, as I follow the *Tour Guide*
My joy didn't come from this world
they can't steal what YAH has given me
After He rebuked that *spirit of depression*
I refuse to go back to the past misery

Cornelius P. Thomas Jr.

Where the Spirit of YAH is, there is liberty
in this freedom, I choose to abide
Never experienced love on this wise
I may stumble, but won't break my stride
My inner man has been strengthened
I only look to my *Source* for assurance
He can restore the weary souls
this "marathon of life" requires endurance
Our mission is simply to represent the *Light of Christ*
in a dark world known as a mental maze
We don't control our next breath or heartbeat
even though YAH can see past today…
Until the end of the age, many will choose
not to trust him
That is until tragedy arises
then prayer becomes the topic of discussion
A brother is born for adversity
enormous pressure has been applied
I want everything that ELOHIYM has for me
every day, my self-will must die!
Called to assume the position on the battlefield
the opposing squad is launching
Fiery darts camouflaged as issues of confusion
hurdles and obstacles, we're overcoming
Seeking to go deeper in this *Word*
so that I can reload and shoot
Not my will, but YAH'S will be done
the *Set apart Spirit* will execute

SOLDIER STORIES: P.O.W.

THE FALLEN SOLDIERS
Isaiah 40:30, Hebrews 11:35-39

In the face of the rival
real soldiers are rarely celebrated
Every living soul under the sun
wants to be appreciated
A man can't prove himself
if not given the chance
Everyone is at war with something
looking to advance
I asked YAH to reprogram my mental state
He's greater than my thought process
Prayers and supplications are continual
I flee from stress to my *Place of Rest*
Many people have died from stress
hoping that their dreams would fall in their laps
The Holy Spirit is my soul's GPS
the Father created the map
On the roads of uncertainty
to find purpose is a must
It is appointed once for a man to die
Ashes to ashes and dust to dust
Dark deception has infiltrated the purpose of men
the curse on the earth
Two dates will appear on every headstone
the dash in between carries the worth
The torch has been passed
therefore I have to go the distance
Forced to get aggressive for my blessings
moving forward with persistence

Cornelius P. Thomas Jr.

Towards a destination
it's either heaven or hell
Soldiers are dropping out of the race
disqualifying themselves
This shouldn't be taking place
everyone was born with a mission
We all have roles to play
tailor-made positions
We all encounter different situations
although we travel similar paths
There is only a limited time
to complete a specific task
Stand up and be counted
we are living in a warzone
I document in remembrance of the *fallen soldiers*
those who are dead and gone
Some have died for the sake of the *Gospel*
others died because they were fed up with living
Many are smothered and choked by their surroundings
countless peers are in prison
You can identify a tree just by watching its fruit
I want my life to speak for me
as I protest in my youth
Part of a mighty troop
the army that answered the heavenly calling
Consumed by the *Consuming Fire*
He will keep me from falling

SOLDIER STORIES: P.O.W.

BATTLE CRIES TO THE BELIEVER
Isaiah 42:13, Joel 2:1

As I stare at the ways of the world
unlimited opportunities are in front of me
The enemy desires to sift me like wheat
because misery loves company
Representing a *Living God* in a dying world
the inhabitants are overtaken by apathy
YAH is training laborers to proclaim the *Good News*
amidst troubled times and catastrophe

All of heaven is backing me
Contending for the faith with a bulldog tenacity
A man's life is full of trouble
We follow the script filled with Kingdom strategies
Because my old life no longer serves me
there's a constant transitioning to evolve
Recipients of abundant grace and mercy
there isn't a problem that God can't solve
No one can travel through life alone
I'm grateful for divine connections
Glorying in these light afflictions
the *Spirit of Truth* will provide directions

This *Word* isn't bound by race, or social status
the light shines amongst all sorts
I seek an abundant life on planet earth
shaped and molded to believe the Lord's report

We have to give place to Holy Spirit

Cornelius P. Thomas Jr.

and refuse to settle for mediocrity
Our actions will expose what we believe
Have to flee from subtle hypocrisy and idolatry
The harvest is plentiful, laborers are few
time is ticking away
We have to make wise choices, watch the signs
and not be selfish when we pray

The enemy seeks to blind side us at every turn
ELOHIYM rebuked the devourer
The blood of the Messiah is against his armies
this is the believer's finest hour
We are more than conquerors through Him that loved us
He destroyed the works of the deceiver
Time to get back what the devil has stolen
my *battle cries to the believer*

MISSING PIECE OF THE PUZZLE
Psalms 71:20-21, Hosea 6:1
Isaiah 3:12

The *Kingdom of God* is inside of me
label me a soul survivor
YAH created a man, strong in posture
a leader, covering, and provider
The new breed of *Abraham's seed*
the defender of the family
The "head of the house" who establishes order
because trouble sparks randomly
Symbolic to Yahshua and the *Church*
whenever I take my wife to be
Then, the two will become one
she will become part of me

Today paints a different picture
men are not in their rightful places
We see genocide, broken homes,
plenty of time wasting and repeated phases
Weary roaming around in circles
most have fallen off track
Our sons grow to mimic our ways
when we never learned how to act

As time ticks away the "Head" has become the prey
approaching family relationships so timidly
Pawning our free will, hiding talents in the earth
trapped as precious commodity of the penitentiary
I know how to express anger

Cornelius P. Thomas Jr.

compassion is far from me
Wives, companions, sons, and daughters
are starving for affection, as long as they get the money
They shouldn't complain about quality time
meanwhile, we remain emotionally distant
I wondered; *why do we live defeated?*
YAH opened my eyes in the same instance

I saw how the devil has cheated
he has tampered with our minds
we began to forsake YAH in exchange for idols
walking dead and spiritually blind
The enemy's background reveals deception
The Sacred Word exposes the truth
We need to pick that up as our weapons
aim at our circumstances and shoot
We're mocked because we left our *Maker*
in ancient times, He made an investment
Have to forsake our own ways to follow the *Messiah*
and begin to learn from life's lessons

As men, we can't afford to give up
learning is a continual process
A journey of a million miles
must begin with a single step of progress
Repent before the *Lamb of YAH*
with your all, seek His face
There's no reward in giving up
the reward is in finishing the race

I represent the restoration of family structure

SOLDIER STORIES: P.O.W.

with a submitted heart posture, graced with endurance
ELOHIYM is my *Shield and Exceeding Great Reward*
He's my *Blessed Assurance*
We win some, we lose some
I flee for shelter in the times of trouble
The man with the *Kingdom of YAH* living on the inside
of him is the *missing piece of the puzzle*

Our families are depending on us
it's too late in the game to fumble
We need the touchdown and the field goal to represent
as sons, brothers, husbands, fathers, and uncles

Cornelius P. Thomas Jr.

END TIME WARRIORS
Zechariah 10:5, 6, John 3:1-10

They say, *"The Holy Ghost is with you.*
He makes your flow so official."
On the low they really feel you
like Nicodemus, then they diss you
In front of a crowd of opinions
peep poetic inventions
In the midst of the storm
journeying through different dimensions
I will stand as The Great *"I AM"*
has given me leeway
Running this race with patience
a lifelong relay
Condemning the loose lips
you know the *"he say, she say"*
Steady rehearsing this *Word*
I keep those verses on replay

End time warriors
isolated like foreigners
YAH'S children die daily
therefore we disregard the coroner
Gotta keep pushing
gotta keep striving
The Almighty provides the cushion
in *His* presence, I'm hiding
Gotta keep grinding
visionary working overtime
So many eyes are blinded

SOLDIER STORIES: P.O.W.

forced to stay military-minded
Gotta keep trying
that's all I know
Endurance wins the race
witness the fiery furnace flow
The just shall live by faith
and the snakes will be exposed
Delivered from the slave mentality
but so many minds are closed

Even though the war is crucial
"Satan, the Lord rebukes you!"
Everyone must choose a side
soldiers have to use the truth to
Shed light on dark corners
speak life in death's valley
The *Light of Christ* that is
the devil desires to have me
We're just a bunch of righteous kids
many times, treated unfairly
The system tries to entice these kids
seems like we're making it barely

Desolate land replenishers
shaped and molded into *Ministers*
We'll either plant or water
then look to the *Author and Finisher*
to bring the increase
The *Holy Spirit* is *He*
who urges me to believe
in what natural eyes cannot see

Cornelius P. Thomas Jr.

(((Spell name)))
L-Y-R-I-C-A-L
G-I-A-N-T
Can't you tell?
That I've been through high water and hell
but still prevailed
Giving honor to the King
to the tree, all sin was nailed
I can remember when I rebelled
before the marvelous *Light* shined
The battles belong to YAH
but the victory is mine

There's hope for the hopeless
in this *Modern Day Babylon*
Due to the optical illusions
it's hard for some to carry on
Gotta keep pushing
gotta keep striving
EL SHADDAI provides the cushion
in His presence, I'm hiding
Gotta keep grinding
visionary working overtime
So many eyes are blinded
forced to stay military-minded

END TIME WARRIORS
Extended

Gotta keep pushing
gotta stay focused
Spectators are looking
in the natural realm, it looks hopeless!
The written *Word* becomes spoken
as I speak life into existence
because of the cross of Jesus Christ
close friends became distant
I press forward with persistence
an artist that moves with precision
The *Set apart Spirit* provides direction
and gives the vision definition

I've been betrayed and snake-bitten
been delayed by hate missions
Murdered by the viper's tongue
"Holy Father, forgive em!"
The Man of Sorrows
became my *Hope* for tomorrow
A God ordained lender
always start off having to borrow
Labeled with the outcasts
my faith causes me to outlast
turbulent winds, vicious attacks, and pain from the past

I represent the warfare in the heat of the sun
YAH is searching for willing vessels
to march to the beat of the drum

Cornelius P. Thomas Jr.

The *Spoken Word* is what I live and breathe
it's what I stand on
When you're seeking to please *EL ELYON*
many times, you'll have to stand alone
He has been there through it all
the good, the bad, and the ugly
I never had a silver spoon
now I have peace as my luxury

The economy is dying
we focus on *Kingdom Building*
This war is for souls
I'm out to recruit lost civilians
Wisdom is justified of her children
this is documentation of the war
The victory is mine
the battle is the Lord's
Witness the poetry bars
from a soldier on a spiritual grind
The battle is YAH'S
the victory is mine

They say, *"The Holy Ghost is with you.
He makes your flow so official."*
On the low, they really feel you
like Nicodemus, then they diss you
In front of a crowd of opinions
peep poetic inventions
In the midst of the storm
journeying through different dimensions
I will stand as The Great *"I AM"*

SOLDIER STORIES: P.O.W.

has given me leeway
Running this race with patience
a lifelong relay
Condemning the loose lips
you know the *"he say, she say"*
Steady rehearsing this *Word*
I keep those verses on replay

End time warriors
isolated like foreigners
YAH'S children die daily
therefore we disregard the coroner

Cornelius P. Thomas Jr.

THROUGH IT ALL, THERE IS HOPE II
Psalms 3:2-6

I will never accept death
I have too much living to do
A purpose to fulfill
a few more giants to kill
Observing activity in the city streets
sin doesn't allow its partakers to enjoy peaceful sleep
Unforgiveness has been planted in those who are mad
with life, bitterness is the root to so much grief!
The *spirit* is rapidly spreading, causing those that are
bound to tread on dangerous grounds
Offenses cause the recipient to anticipate the big payback

We will never grow holding grudges against one another
When I look into your life, I see similarities of my life
one in the same, yet fearfully and wonderfully made
If a man falls into a ditch, his neighbor should extend
a helping hand to deliver him
Sooner or later, they may switch places
instead, the hidden issues inside will cause the neighbor
to talk down on the man that has fallen
Jealousy, envy, insecurities, strife, and division

The miracle called "life" provides unseen opportunities
I seek spiritual growth and emotional stability
the chance to unify among the brethren
should not go overlooked
I have heard that there is strength in numbers
Surely, unlimited power is available

SOLDIER STORIES: P.O.W.

when we get on one accord
One mind and one common goal
There's power in prayer
the results are found in Jesus' name
As we search for peace
we're often confronted by confusion
We have to look closely and discern the trickery
many are lost in a mental maze and optical illusions

Bitterness has deep roots that stem from
mistakes that were made, chances that were never taken,
or betrayal from a trusted source
Maybe, we all are victims of prior tragedies
many people wish that they could turn back
the hands of time
However, time doesn't wait for anyone!

There is hope among the land of the living
an opportunity to get it right and learn from the wrongs
Only YAH can save us!
The Possessor of Heaven and Earth
Eternal destinations are tied to decisions
that we make in this present life
Many sit and wonder; *do dreams really come true?*
There is healing in the land
as we activate faith, we have to stand
In the heat of the day, there is constant battle
the *Poet* is caught in between those who live by faith
and those who live by their emotions
I am determined to bring a positive message
filled with substance and hope

Cornelius P. Thomas Jr.

A journey of a million miles
must begin with a single step
However, many are paralyzed and nearsighted
slaves to impulse decisions
they will make pit stops their destinations

Through all of the trials, falsehood, and deceit
Today there is hope
this gives us the power to defeat
Any obstacle that comes our way
even the *enemy within*
I will never accept death
YAH has made it possible for us to win
through Mashiach our Savior

SOLDIER STORIES: P.O.W.

REPORTING LIVE FROM THE SCENE
Isaiah 51:20, Hosea 4:1-3, 6-7

I'm posted up on this jobsite
in the middle of a drug zone
These dudes are strapped with their mug on
some are plotting, trying to make their plugs strong
Study long study wrong
in the hood it's the same ole song
In my mind I am free
although the mental is a constant warzone
"What y'all smoking on?"
that's what I hear a young man ask
For me, that's a thing of the past
flashing out ready to blast
I don't hide behind a mask
I just offer advice
I remember when *I was that young man*
now I seek to be productive in life

Our only way out is Jesus Christ
between ELOHIYM and man, He's the *Door*
YAH can provide wisdom and knowledge to the simple
give wealth to mentalities that are poor
We war within ourselves
at the core, the war is always spiritual
The conflict often hides behind problems and issues
if you're hurting, I'm probably feeling you

It takes muscle to hustle
in the home of the brave

Cornelius P. Thomas Jr.

Some hustles will lead to trouble
witness the *home of the slaves*
Jesus is *the Way, the Truth, and the Life*
Today is filled with opportunity
Satan leads astray, we shoot and fight
bringing down the property value in the communities
Whatever happened to unity?
...one accord, you and me?
Every man is for himself
in the face of knowledge, there's so much truancy
Living defeated
the youngsters are into way more than getting weeded
Chasing after these idols
the set-up is strategic
Divine intervention is needed
Sometimes, our mouths, we should keep them
shut and conquer regret
Identify what's true, and seek *Him*

We have to get up, stand up
and cease from complaining
Jesus came that we may live abundant lives
I refuse to settle for just maintaining
YAH will increase my greatness
and comfort me on every side
I refuse to break my stride
even though pressure has been applied
Daily, my flesh must die
you can hear the sorrow in the sighs
We've become immune to the tears that mothers cry
when they lose their kids to street ties

SOLDIER STORIES: P.O.W.

The pain is hard to hide as I scribble
I know that each day we can progress a little
We all have freedom of choice
I chose life and still, caught in the middle
In the middle of a warzone
in the hood, we can't walk off and leave our cars on
Lord, help us through the storms
because morals are too far gone!

Everyone is grinding to look the part
most will never notice the subtle deception
Those of us who embrace the *Uncompromised Truth*
must be ready to face rejection
I went from street fame to looked upon as lame
due to mental prisons, filled with confusion
Many people will stay in bondage to their problems
because they despise the *Solution*
As long as YAH has my back
you will find me on the frontline
Reporting live from the scene
unedited versions found in the rhymes

Cornelius P. Thomas Jr.

PLAYING FOR KEEPS
Romans 8:31

Went from drug and alcohol dependency
to the knowledge of the truth
YAH has supplied clarity and illumination
for my heart and mind
He has committed all things unto *His* Son
Jesus Christ (Yahusha Ha'Mashiach)
All He wants is our trust
He is *Faithful and True*
The spirits that once held me captive
no longer have dominion over me
They are eager to kill me
because I promote what they hate
The true doctrine of Christ
They hover around in the air
seeking to use any willing vessel
Assigned attacks come against me

The *Lamb's Blood* on my forehead
is a stamp that proves I'm a foreigner among the masses
Strategic battles take place on a continual basis
the wicked continues to plot against the righteous
*Why is it that the systems of the world can come
together to keep the masses in bondage?*
Meanwhile the *Church*, as a whole, remains divided
due to the subtle spirits of compromise
A house divided cannot stand!
The chosen vessels have been given power to overcome
we shouldn't be ignorant to the wicked devices

SOLDIER STORIES: P.O.W.

The level of focus is distorted
*Why is there so much confusion among those
who supposed to possess Resurrection Power?*
Demons have committed themselves to the task
of blinding the eyes and perverting the minds
of the masses
They infiltrate mental capacities and persuade people
to engage in riotous living
We, as soldiers for the *Kingdom of ELOHIYM* must be
willing to stand boldly upon the *ROCK* in which we trust
…even in the face of death

Passive, carnal minded believers
will miss their visitation
Tenacious, courageous, and patient
Meek, discreet, and elite should be words that describe
the believer's character
Jesus said that *His sheep know His voice and a
stranger's voice, they will not follow*
This means that we have to possess a spiritual ear
and spiritual eyes that have 20/20 vision
Spiritual eyes of discernment
I will stand as royalty
I will not bow down and serve these dumb idols
Jesus defeated everything that we will ever face
We can shout the victory, we are not victims of sin
No weapon formed against us shall prosper
I possess this delegated authority
because I abide in the *Secret Place*
The devil cannot overstep the boundaries of the *Blood*
we are in a war and both sides are playing for keeps

Cornelius P. Thomas Jr.

CITY UNDER SIEGE
Matthew 24:6-8

We spread love not hate
with wise counsel, we make war
It's not as important to be accepted as it is
to discover purpose and raise the bar
So many atrocities
nations are in an uproar and angry
Racial divide as demons hide
behind the scenes, placing blame see
Mainly due to injustice
we don't trust them, they don't trust us
Bloodshed has the masses scared
the enemy can attack when it's "just us"
A fatherless generation
replacing YAH with idols
The land is disquieted
protesting and rioting in the name of survival
Some call Him *"Father Time"*
some equate the divine with *"Mother Nature"*
From generation to generation
we must acknowledge the *Creator*
The world's *Savior*
we're all in need of saving grace
Human life has no value
bodies are disposed like waste
There's still time left to seek His face
repentance is required before revival
The people are oppressed by the deceiver
while many discredit the Bible

SOLDIER STORIES: P.O.W.

There's a healing at hand
but war has to take place first
It takes faith to expect the supernatural
in the natural realm, it's getting worse
We spread love not hate
with wise counsel, we make war
It's not as important to be accepted as it is
to discover purpose and take it far
Many have been taught to only call on YAH
when tragedy arises
Once things are fine, idols are welcomed back
spirits of deception are wearing disguises
Only YAH can ease the pain
as emotions are flaring and order is disrupted
He's a *Place of Shelter* in times of trouble
due to corruption, focus has been abducted
Some choose to protest and march
while others pray for warring angels to be loosed
Justice is a daily discussion
Who's willing to pluck hatred at the root?
There's a lack of trust and respect for authorities
racism is embraced by the majority
The agenda of the hidden hands are in motion
this tempestuous storm wasn't welcomed cordially
The land is disquieted
families bereaved can't properly grieve
I poetically breathe as the ink bleeds
the city is under siege

Cornelius P. Thomas Jr.

LIGHT AFFLICTIONS
2 Corinth 4:17, Romans 8:18

I will push through the trouble
I will press beyond the pain
The Lord is my portion forever
through it all, He reigns
I rejoice at the *Word*
as one that has found great spoils
The righteous covenant is still valid
longing to forget all of my toil
*Why attempt to climb a mountain, when I can speak
to it and it be removed?*
Faith without works is dead
seems like we have the concept confused
Woke up and fled to my *Resting Place*
I have ceased from my own works
The ELOHIYM who knew me from my mother's belly
has predestined the *True Church*
Label me as a Revolutionary
regardless of what they tell me
Radically confessing the *Word*
because I know He'll never fail me
They still reject the truth
Jesus was rejected of men
A *Friend* who sticks closer than a brother
guess one could say He's my next of kin
Thankful for the *Spirit of Adoption*
whereby we cry *Abba Father*
Refuse to let my eyes deceive me
in the natural, things got harder

SOLDIER STORIES: P.O.W.

Supernatural promises await me
so many people think that I'm crazy
I write these letters like a "mad man"
knowing that the blessings will overtake me
While many continue to underrate me
in my *Rock and Ark of Safety*
There's peace that passes understanding
demonic attacks cannot break me!
Opinions of men cannot shake me
they didn't choose or validate me
The *Defender of my Soul*
is the same *One* who will allocate me
My faith will activate *He*
the Beginning and the End
I confidently suffer these light afflictions
because my *Battle Fighter* will avenge
me of my adversaries
He rose and gave gifts to men
when I raise the "*Blood Stained Banner*"
He will show up to defend
Therefore I can rejoice
many are the afflictions of the righteous
The wheat and tares must grow together
the imposters may look like us
But, the *Deliverer* is on the scene
the *Life Giver* overthrows the schemes
before seeds of deception are planted into the thought
process, He will manifest Godly visions and dreams

TRANSFORMING THROUGH THE TRANSITION

CAN'T BE ALL THINGS
Ephesians 4:7

You can't be "all things" to all people
Have to "do you" on this journey
because hidden motives can be deceitful
Don't try to save the world
we already have *One* who did that
They still don't believe Him
everyone is enlightened and have the facts
At least we think we got it all together
smiling faces will wish you well
As soon as you walk away
they're placing bets with hopes that you fail
We all want to go to heaven
but struggle to let go of hell
They'll run your business in the ground
when it comes to theirs, they don't "kiss and tell"
There was one dude that sung a song
"Life is like a wishing well"
I say that life is a gamble
Who's really taking risks to fail?
We all have specific purposes
born to fulfill an assignment
We have a responsibility to know the truth
if we seek, we can find it
Attacks are launched for me to throw in the towel
yet, still I rise
The *Preserver of Life* dwells within me
I will not die!
A threat to these busters

Cornelius P. Thomas Jr.

the unseen enemies that are deceiving nations
With faith "out of this world"
an alien taught to embrace patience
I AM my greatest competition
the opinions of others really don't matter
Praying that blinded eyes would be opened
within these series of disasters
The sign of the times
the beginning of sorrows
Most people are trying to make it through today
they can't even visualize tomorrow
Will you lend, beg, or borrow?
We all must choose a side
Who do you trust?
Let us discuss, because we all have a *Guide*
Dodging fiery darts, because they shoot to kill
a man of faith rebuking fear
On the enemy's hit list as a fugitive
sometimes, the struggle is too for real
There's an assignment at hand
can't be "all things" to all people
They hated Christ without a cause
the reason I use my *Weapon* like it's lethal

SOLDIER STORIES: P.O.W.

LIFT UP A STANDARD
Isaiah 59:19

I cannot accept defeat
I just wasn't built like that
Never ran from a battle, got knocked down
and didn't fight back
That was in the natural realm
predestined to be a *Giant* in the Spirit
Extreme warfare on every side
my vibe, circumstances can't kill it
Joy is found in YAH'S presence
in the midst of weakness, He's my strength
This life is so uncertain
filled with trouble, anguish, and suspense

When your dwelling place is the dunghill
it can get scandalous on the battlefield
Find me warring for my covenant rights so that the next
generation can benefit in my latter years
Today the battle is underway
my faith is activated, so I'm unafraid
The *Word of the Lord* guides my footsteps
guaranteed to overcome these days
Way more than *twelve years of a slave*
the common state of the environment
Deception is embraced like precious jewels
some Shepherds are exposed as Hirelings
I've been tempted to turn back
but I'm in too deep in this love affair
Flames are ignited inside of me

Cornelius P. Thomas Jr.

a built-in-compass to overcome the snares

Some say, *"The Holy Ghost is with you.*
He makes your flow so official."
He stirs the gift to uplift
He provides hope for hopeless issues
Kingdom building underground
because I can hear the sound
Of abundance, it's surely coming
the depths of salvation are profound
The *Miracle Worker* is on the scene
The *Self Existent, Great Physician*
His grace and mercy is extended to all men
as He speaks, we have to listen
Those with an ear to hear
the *still small voice* filled with instructions
My heavenly account is piling up
can't afford to have any deductions
as I call it down from heaven
The *Word* is forever settled
with faith greater than a mustard seed
YAH will lift up a standard against the devil

WITH HOPES TO DELIVER
Isaiah 10:27, Hebrews 11:1

Effective rhymes are delivered
with hopes to deliver
Wasn't born in a little tent
but Earl K. Long Hospital was located by the river
It's been too hard living
however I'm not afraid to die
On this faith-walk, we die daily
for the sake of ADONAI

How you gonna win if you ain't right within?
If you're not in the right position
How can He show up to defend?
Persecution keeps me motivated
and I know they hate it
I am so related to the struggles like your fam
I AM the greatest!
Did you just read what was said?
I AM IS THE GREATEST
I AM my greatest competition
the worlds were created
By the words of *His* mouth
this means we have the power
To create our own world
the victory is ours

If we fall off in the days of adversity
we have no strength
Let the weak say that I'm strong

Cornelius P. Thomas Jr.

in the midst of the suspense
During chaotic times and perverted rhymes
the *Living God* is still moving
Keep your focus placed on Him
even when the journey seems confusing

You cannot reason with a demon
familiar *spirits* will try to keep you entangled
Spectators think I'm just babbling off
as I embrace the *Spirit of Truth* and these mighty angels
Loose lips talked about me in this season of testing
witnessed a temporary "fall off"
Soldier Stories are recorded precisely
I'll document until I'm hauled off

Truth is that we all can do better
by no means am I better
Seeking to be consumed by this *Power*
to the *Spirit of Life*, I'm a debtor
Still here due to mercy and grace
laced with favor and game
At least that's the stereotype
I call it a transition or change
Eternal life is my aim
already crowned with the victory
Totally depending on the *Holy Spirit*
He is my *Liberty*

BOLD EXPRESSION
Ephesians 3:12

No mediocre
we are children of the Kingdom
Bound by the *Spirit of Truth*
boldly we express our freedom
How can one begin again?
That's the question
If it doesn't have any substance
we have to turn a deaf ear to suggestions
The things that we're facing right now
one day, will be a thing of the past
Witness the ecclesiastical flow
the only thing that will last
or withstand the test of time
Just as the sun was blessed to shine
YAH'S *Word* will accomplish its mission
I AM next in line
To receive the covenant blessings
more of what He has in store for me
Emotionally at my wit's end
but this isn't the end of the story
It doesn't matter who believes in me
as long as I believe in me
We are children of the Kingdom
who desire to see the people free
Embracing a heavenly perception
the Covenant is valid and equally
Distributed among the recipients
we seek to live peaceably

Cornelius P. Thomas Jr.

Withdrawn because of the *Truth*
nevertheless summoned to speak the truth
For a moment, had to regroup
reshaped, remolded, refueled
By the *Master's touch*, my mind renewed
all due to the *Living Word*
Faith comes by hearing
but some have never heard
About this relationship uncompromised
this causes us to run from lies
The subtle deception of the enemy controlling the masses
disgruntled minds
Thanks be unto YAH
He always causes me to triumph
No matter what the trials of life throw at me
I remain defiant
We cannot bow to the enemy's tactics
as children of the Kingdom
Bound by the *Spirit of Truth*
boldly we express our freedom
No mediocre
enlisted as YAHUAH'S soldiers
Taking it one day at a time
before the game of life is over

CROSSING OVER
Joshua 1:11

God's love is unconditional
gives me vision transitional
He is a God of encounters
that we may flee from the rituals
He desires sacred worship, not traditional
we disregard what we see in the physical
So many upsets and let downs
but I'm still expecting miracles
The times are chaotic and terrible
the *Word of Life* holds true
We have to leave the past behind
in order to press forward towards the new
It's hard to say farewell to what was
so many tears have been shed
Productive memories live within my heart
even though yesterday is dead
I decree an abundant life
because an abundant life has been promised
I want everything that was ordained
wasted time, I can't stomach
Spiritual ears must be keen to hear His voice
want to be in tune with *His* heartbeat
The *Seed,* the *Promise*, and the *Supernatural*
I can rest in my *Peace*
Jesus is *His* name
I raise my *Banner* to show blood stains
My *Protection* in a diseased world
the inhabitants are going insane

Cornelius P. Thomas Jr.

The time has come to cross over
deliverance showed up at the intersection
Listening closely for instructions
the journey is incomplete without directions
Worship is essential
in order to get to the next dimension
Greedy for more of God's presence
I reverence my *Redemption*
He is the *Great Physician*
He'll arise with healing in His wings
I bow my heart before the King
unconventional praises as I sing
He is purging me through the pain
testimonies ooze from battle wounds
I surrender my own agenda
as I remember those gone too soon
However, the journey must continue
partaker of a great awakening
Awaiting the manifestation of miracles
already in place for men
God's love is unconditional
gives me vision transitional
He is a God of encounters
that we may flee from the rituals

SOLDIER STORIES: P.O.W.

A HEAVENLY PERCEPTION
Ephesians 2:6, Colossians 3:1-2

For all I trust him *(faith)*
"Dear ELOHIYM, give me peace!"
Within these troubled times
troubled spirits make men weak
Praise has to be uttered
purpose has to be discovered
In the midst of the storm
Yahusha sticks closer than a brother

A brother is born for adversity
the growing pains are hurting me
Attempting to disrupt my *peace of mind*
as they murder me verbally
I'll die before I give in to fear
it sets the stage for doubt and unbelief
I expect a supernatural increase
miracles and a divine release

Warfare is daily
though He slay me, yet will I trust Him
A man's belly shall be satisfied by the fruit of his mouth
confessions with deep substance
The spirit of pride comes against me
I desperately cry out to my *Savior*
He's my *Eternal Companion*
My prosperity and favor
I risk it all as a risk-taker
a *Kingdom of YAH* representer

Cornelius P. Thomas Jr.

Called to soar like an eagle
won't even send negative words back to the sender
I don't have time
the borrowed purpose is divine
The *Light* dwells inside of me
sometimes I can't see the shine

You can feel my heart beating on each line
if you tune in to the dark sayings
Words classified as *Proverbs*
in a hopeless state if debating
Back and forth determines my worth
I already know who *I AM*
May not see it in the natural just yet
the *Blood of the Lamb* causes me to stand
In season or out of season
angels war against demons
Trying to prevent our petitions from manifesting
I'm thankful for the air that I'm breathing

Embracing my dominion to exercise
authority over the enemy
I'd rather be content than covetous
with a heavenly perception and sacred identity
The remedy for hating is love
the core of my identity is love
This can't be obtained by human abilities
I have to trust in that *Love*
YAHUAH ELOHIYM is love
love covers a multitude of sins
Imperfect and unworthy

SOLDIER STORIES: P.O.W.

still predestined to win
Because of the *Sacrifice*
my life has become a sacrifice
Darkness shows up in the daytime
in a hopeless state if you're lacking Christ

For all I trust him *(faith)*
"Dear ELOHIYM, give me peace!"
Within these troubled times
troubled spirits make men weak
When I am weak, I am strong
YAH'S grace is sufficient
He's guaranteed to right the wrongs
He daily loads us with benefits

Cornelius P. Thomas Jr.

THE EMERGENCY ALERT SYSTEM
Daniel 12:4, 2 Tim 3:7, Jude 1:15-16

Effective leaders are those who've diligently followed
no one can alter YAH'S plan
As I tune in to follow His commands
persecution arises to hinder my stand
Experiencing turbulence in the spirit realm
but I hold up my *"Blood Stained Banner"*
I will not abort my purpose on earth for men
that will die in like manner
The *Word of YAH* will prevail
because this *Word* is pure and true
We'll get back what the devil has stolen
reparations are due
My brother's wrath is kindled against me
he doesn't understand liberation
The devil seeks to divide and conquer
witness the separation
Many are uplifted in pride
victims of the devil's penetration
Some seek to prostitute YAH'S word
a wicked and adulterous generation
Many try to discredit the name of Jesus
I see division due to tradition
They embrace certain doctrines and denounce others
beefing over religion
The land of the free, the home of the brave
in their minds, most are slaves
Vanity is taken to extreme measures
Who can escape the blaze?

SOLDIER STORIES: P.O.W.

Those who repent and seek the *"True God"*
instead religion, tradition, and superstition swirls
All devils see is division and big business
my Kingdom is not of this world!
Souls are lost and they're hurting
seducing spirits are flirting
Jesus is my *Dwelling Place*
the place where I can cast my burdens
YAHWEH has given simple commandments
most of them are thrown out the door
Conscious intellect has replaced love
hearts are hardened deep within the core
The vast majority of this generation is walking dead
Satan is destroying with a deceitful touch
Destruction has overtaken the masses
we can blame idolatry and lust
There is a way that seems right to man
but the end of that way is death
Many profess to possess head knowledge
on the *knowledge of the Truth*, many have slept
The wolves in sheep's clothing are creeping
spiritual gang banging and beefing
I flee to my hiding place in order to hear YAH speaking
Precious life spans are leaking
the days are wasting away
The thief is constantly deceiving
leading the masses astray
We give the devil too much credit
He's the villain in everybody's story
demons war for territory
The believer has power over worry

Cornelius P. Thomas Jr.

The *Eternal ELOHIYM* is in control
due to free will, He allows
The human to choose life or death
don't get caught living in denial
Dwelling in the *Beginning of Sorrows*
some fruit is forbidden
My life is hidden in the Messiah
the *Glorified Savior* has risen
For sins, there is remission
forgiveness for those seeking change
Both sides are playing for keeps
souls are on the line in this game
Time is ticking away
have to make the ultimate choice before time is up
Choose salvation or damnation
the paths that we travel will define us
I shout the victory
delivered from being an abused victim
Warfare is continuous
I continue to sound the *Emergency Alert System*

SOLDIER STORIES: P.O.W.

THE STRUGGLE CONTINUES
2 Corinth 11:22-33, 12:1-10, Hebrews 11:36-40

I can hear the cries of the Prophets and righteous men
that have gone before me
They were forced to embrace their pilgrimage
due to the oppression in this wicked land
Ordained before the world's foundation to take a stand
Father YAH, *Most High*, is greater than the opposition
The *Creator* will avenge the blood of His servants that
was shed for righteousness' sake
Without the burden of carrying the cross
there can be no victory of obtaining the crown
Salvation isn't based upon feelings
the just shall live by faith
I am married to destiny
I refuse to cheat on her
I will not utter the words *"separation"* or *"divorce"*
The Blood of the Lamb has formed the covenant
the Covenant has been stamped with the seal of approval
from *The Most High*
This is documentation of my life's issues
sacred studies, military-minded strategies
and the poetic revolution
Greater is *He* that is within me than he that's in the world
EL Roi, the strong ELOHIYM who sees is my defense
The *Ruach Ha'Qodesh* is the Governor
of YAH'S Kingdom
Take heed to the warnings, intricate plots, future plans,
revelation knowledge and prophecies
all composed in a poetic form

Cornelius P. Thomas Jr.

Much more than human intellect, being led by feelings,
or a natural point-of-view or ideas
The sacrifice among my peers
my heavenly reward will never disappear
Therefore, I must stand strong!
Associated with the *Greatest*
He anointed these phrases, clauses, and pronouns
I'm no more than an earthen vessel
this makes the mission profound
Holy Spirit is a *Genius*
all-powerful and all-knowing
We must lose in order to win
How can I remain ordinary and just blend in?
The cross of the Messiah was the entrance gate
the blood stain on my forehead proves
that I'm in too deep
A Kingdom Ambassador on divine assignment
until my flesh takes its eternal sleep
Even then will these words live on
then some listening ear will hear my cries

THAT I MAY KNOW HIM
Philippians 3:10

The splendor of a King
from the throne come heavenly strategies
I bow before the *Creator of all things*
clothed with power and majesty
Great is His faithfulness
His mercy endures forever
I embrace the *fruits of the Spirit*
so that I may know Him better
Suffering through these afflictions
the *Comforter* is present in any condition
I cry out to the *Great Physician*
placed in position to listen
To what the Spirit is saying to the *Church*
want to know Him in the power of His resurrection
and the fellowship of His sufferings
He is my *Protection*
Sealed unto the day of redemption
engraved in the Almighty's palm
It's impossible for Him to forsake His own inheritance
forced to weather the storms
There's nothing short about His arms
His eyes are upon the righteous
In this world, we shall be hated
Who cares if they don't like us?
We have the victory
even when it doesn't feel like it
Salvation isn't based on feelings
as I hear it, I write it

Cornelius P. Thomas Jr.

I refuse to be controlled by my emotions
or live out of my own mind
Feelings are real, but the mind can play tricks
can't afford to stumble like those blind
Been down that road before
through any element, I'll spit it raw
Constantly asking YAH to open my eyes
that I may behold wondrous things out of His law
He is Set apart. He is *Sovereign.*
He is omnipotent and transcendent
It's not His will that anyone should perish
I've been branded with the remnant
The Word of ELOHIYM isn't bound
the *Word* is what I have hidden in my heart
I stand on this same *Word*
when it's all good or when trouble sparks
I AM healed by the *Word*
I was saved by the *Word*
The *Word* is my lethal weapon
He set me free as a bird
Flying in an open heaven
with my hands lifted to the sky
Endurance wins the race
but patience is despised
…among this generation

SOLDIER STORIES: P.O.W.

BALLADS OF A FOREIGN SOLDIER
Ephesians 5:19

A lonely heart can be shattered
a comforted heart can beat freely
A broken heart can ruin love at its best state
an evil heart can deceive thee
Who can understand the motives within one's heart?
...besides the ELOHIYM of all flesh?
He's the Father of the *Elect*
the only One to provide rest

Whether one is caged in a jail cell, stationed in an area
living in solitude or the barracks
We long to be accepted or appreciated
in different relationships, especially marriage
Soldiers need reassurance
while marching on foreign soil
We should never invest our all into immediate
gratification, YAH can train soldiers to be loyal

The things that we think are sure
can turn out to be seasonal
Intimate encounters with our *Maker*
can lead to joy unspeakable
When we fail to listen to the Spirit
our actions proceed as relentless
We look for love in all of the wrong places
trying to uphold a certain image
Instead of having a heart of repentance
we trust human logic that is fluctuating

Cornelius P. Thomas Jr.

Then EL has to break through the barriers of fear
doubt and frustration
Let's love on the *God of all creation*
find our confidence and embrace patience
We all are in need of pure love
and this is found through salvation
Contending for our faith in this war
because this world is not our home
In pursuit of the King, feeling home sick
but He will never leave us alone
So far out of my comfort zone
the things that I've gained are counted as loss
Blessed in the city, blessed in the field
still called to carry my cross

Healed in my mind and body
emotionally balanced and whole
In all things, there's a process
life or death attached to any story that's told
Often tempted with the pride of life
urged to embrace temporary pleasure
However, I AM married to destiny
YAH and I will always be together
Seasons and people change
but He blesses beyond measure
I couldn't appreciate true success
if I never was acquainted with failure
The *Word*, Spirit, and gesture
reveals that I'm an alien in this land
The Ballads of a Foreign Soldier
many won't understand

CONDITIONING
1 Corinth 9:24-27, 1 Tim 4:7-8

Summoned to deliver effective lyrics of poetry
at times, I feel so disconnected
In a world where I seek to encourage others
on the receiving end, I'm being neglected
The stirring of the Holy Spirit has been resurrected
chastisement takes place within my being
Urged to practice what I preach
believing is seeing
I was given grace to record these testimonies
but these letters don't belong to me
My life is not my own
from vain opinions, we have to stay free
I search diligently for balance
The great move among the *Household of Faith* will not
prosper, unless we stay in agreement
with the marching orders
In the midst of a foreign land
a soldier can easily lose his way
Some would rather slander their neighbors
than to stand in the gap and pray
This process is not cute
We, as disciples must be willing to submit
and yield to the *Spirit of YAH*
There is no other way that we will see
the God-given visions manifest
In the past, when I was under strenuous pressure
I unknowingly sought after other avenues by which I
could attain the promises

Cornelius P. Thomas Jr.

Taking matters into "my own" hands
only to discover that I was going in circles
I cannot speak to it, if I did not go through it
Training and conditioning on a continual basis
being pruned and purged, stripped, and refined
The resistance doesn't feel good
the pressure from the trials produces power to endure
Insecurities cannot threaten intense determination
the *spirit of fear* tries to mock me
My faith in YAH is greater
than what I am going through
To whom much is given, much is required
in order to go through the fire
you must have the proper attire
At times, I want to turn in my resignation
and flee from the assignment
Yet, I was chosen and I'm already in too deep
Yahshua paid the price for the *lost sheep*
Those who follow Him must pay a price
the denial of self
This means transforming from selfishness to selflessness
Individually, as well as collectively, we have to embrace
self-worth, and even that worth has to line up with
our God-given identities
I write and speak it, as I hear it, live it, and see it
My life is at stake every time I speak in this great Name
we must sanctify ELOHIYM in everything that we do
This is the reason
for continuous training and conditioning
All of the promises of YAH are mine
the *Words* spoken over my life cannot return void

SOLDIER STORIES: P.O.W.

THE SET-UP
Philippians 1:28-29, 2:1-4

Today, I am really in tune with my true identity
The cause and effect of situations
are so crucial and transparent
The enormous pressure from the trials that I'm facing
will help someone else down the road
The battles have become more intense
than when I first began this faith-walk
Often faced with hardships and troubles
that some couldn't survive
YAH'S strength is made perfect in my weakness
Sicknesses and uncommon symptoms
have tried to infiltrate my body
The devil and his cohorts seek to utterly destroy me
nevertheless, healing is the *children's bread*
I seek the wisdom of ELOHIYM which is ranked
far above the world's restraints
I am deeply rooted in this spiritual war
I embrace the privilege to represent EL SHADDAI
my self-will has become obsolete
Often confronted with the lust of the unclean
we will not overcome the battles in our own strength
Jesus Christ
is my *Source* and *Shield*
Who can search the deep, hidden, radical things of YAH?
Only the *Spirit of YAH*
No one can understand my innermost struggles,
except the *Savior* who took my afflictions
and infirmities to the tree

Cornelius P. Thomas Jr.

Times and seasons are ordained
Who can race and outrun the clock on the wall?
As long as the earth remains
there shall be seed time and harvest
From the dust did man come forth
and to the dust shall man return
Therefore I run to the *Creator of Time*
Even though there's a war in my members
ultimately, a stranger's voice, I will not follow
I had to become acquainted with failure
in order to appreciate true success
My "frienemies" lay private snares for my feet
anxiously anticipating my downfall
YAHUAH-Shammah, the omnipresent ELOHIYM
is aware
He reveals His secrets to His children
He will fill the vessels that thirst for *Living Waters*!
Circumstances have no power
in the piercing eyes of faith
Just because we've been delayed
doesn't mean that we've been denied
All things work together for the good of those who love
ELOHIYM, those who are the called according
to His purpose
It is all a set-up
we call it the appointed time
Our lives are complete in Him
the branches connected to the *True Vine*

SOLDIER STORIES: P.O.W.

THE VERBAL ASSASSIN
Proverbs 18:21

The gunshots fly at random
it seems like we're losing
Everyone is searching for answers
but don't agree on the solution
Jesus Christ is the *Hope of Glory*
in the midst of confusion
Satan desires to keep us distracted
deceived by delusions
In the middle of a storm
the wrong path has been corrected
Always prepared to go to war
but the cause was misdirected
What the devil intends for evil
YAH turns it around for our good
It takes discipline and strategic action to overcome
the statistics placed on the hood
We forget to be compassionate as long as the
circumstances don't involve us
The devil's power is limited
but can be magnified through disorder
Behind enemy lines
we have to fight to make a difference
Lack of knowledge is a downfall
pride and arrogance, mixed with ignorance
My job is to speak *Word* to your spirit
so your heart can feel me when you hear it
I am thankful for gifts and talents
fruits of the Spirit found in the lyrics

Cornelius P. Thomas Jr.

Some people have been abandoned by support systems
others are labeled as rejects and outcasts
We eventually learn to lean on *Everlasting Arms*
Jesus, the *First and the Last*
The race is not given to the swift
please, stop moving so fast!
Life consists of so much more
than laboring for cash
As we race in the heat of the day
be aware that there's only a limited time
The *Life Giver* wants all of us to choose life
the deception in this world won't limit this rhyme
The system will try to tame us
ELOHIYM has made countless attempts to train us
Rulers of society stamp us with labels
a righteous anger is present to discern the angles
I won't take the bait and participate in the genocide
instead, I'll elevate my mind
Seeking wisdom, knowledge, and understanding
that can open the eyes of those blind
Success is a learned behavior
unwavering faith requires action
I'm grateful for the true knowledge
that I am fruit from Christ's passion
I decrease that He may increase
this world has temporary satisfaction
I represent the *Eternal Truth*
call me a *Verbal Assassin*

SOLDIER STORIES: P.O.W.

CRIES OF ANGUISH
Psalms 22

Predestined to overcome
feel like a walking time bomb
The just shall live by faith
have to wait until the appointed time comes
Psychological warfare
their job is to promote mental slavery
My mind belongs to YAH
"Sorry, don't have any vacancies!"

Liken this script to my closet
the pen is my freedom from skeletons
When I look in the mirror
I can see strength beyond the melanin
Resilient perception from within
fleeing from anything that isn't relevant
To where I'm headed not where I've been
steps were ordered by YAH'S intelligence

Feels like I'm emotionally slipping away
but I refuse to quit fighting
Deaf ears turn into cold shoulders
but I refuse to quit writing
A heart full of aspirations
witnessing a lack of salutations
Whenever you choose to trust *The Most High*
you disconnect from man's validation

The *"so called"* love is fake

Cornelius P. Thomas Jr.

yet, the secret hate is so real
The pain seems unbearable
the joy of YAH is my shield
Or should I say my Source of Strength?
A lack of compassion is the norm
Many are deceived by trends and fashion
never notice the purpose within the storms
There are some that I thought would be here
they are gone but not forgotten
Betrayed and abandoned by those in my household
evil spirits are plotting

Psychological warfare
for instructions I have to listen
With expectations to be fruitful
in the land of my afflictions
We win some, we lose some
fell victim to subtle attacks
Had to learn how to pick my battles
for a moment, my purpose was snatched

Feeling grateful at the royal table
because I don't deserve a chair
Thankful that Jesus nailed it all to the tree
His attributes are rare
The Most High is nothing like mankind
His thoughts are above human comparison
The ELOHIYM *of all Creation* restores my soul
in life's marathon

In a time where holiness is tainted

SOLDIER STORIES: P.O.W.

by religion and entertainment
As for me, quitting is not an option
so I expose my *Cries of Anguish*

Cornelius P. Thomas Jr.

THE GATEWAY
John 10:9, 14:6

Used to be naughty by nature
with a rude behavior
After all I've been through, I'm still here
far from a faker
Inspiration is freely given
in the land of the takers
The Father gave *His* only begotten
but the deception lurking is major
The hell raisers
cannot stop the plan of God
They choose lies as their truth and the proof
is camouflaged
The Lamb of God
is the only *Gateway* to heaven
The *Captain of the Hosts* will train us
how to effectively use our weapons
Speak the *Word* into the atmosphere
choosing faith over fear
As we await the prophetic rain
our redemption is drawing near
In the midst of chaotic times
YAH is still great
He is greatly to be praised
as the world prepares to meet its fate
At the name of Jesus, every knee shall bow
and every tongue will confess
that He is the *Door* or *Gateway*
to truly living life blessed

SOLDIER STORIES: P.O.W.

Seems like I'm hanging on by a thread
tried by the *Word of the Lord*
That thread is my *Lifeline, my Source*
my *Umbilical Cord*
He's the reason I stand in the midst of war
circumstances show up like a bully
Making threats like promises won't manifest
but subtle deception can't pull me
From this supernatural love affair
greater than any human connection
Promotion doesn't come from rubbing elbows
while the *Gateway* is in intercession
I make my requests known
as He cries out for *His Body*
and those He will bring into the sheepfold
These spirits try to divide the
remnant who will not bow down
scattered across the four winds of the earth
Can't reach the Father without the Son
He's the *Gateway*, the *Head of the Church*
Used to be naughty by nature
with a rude behavior
Transformed as I entered the *Gateway*
He's also known as the *Savior*

Cornelius P. Thomas Jr.

PRISONER OF WAR II
2 Chronicles 20:15, 2 Corinth 10:3-5

A prisoner of war called to stand
when circumstances seem unfavorable
Gifted by the *Supreme Being*
these devils can't penetrate this flow
The flow of the anointing
nor the flow of these rhymes
Attacks are launched from every angle
but I pay the attacks no mind
Studying to be quiet
unless it's a confession of what the *Word* says
Hoping that the listening ear will be edified
as I make the most of each day

I lift my hands to *The Most High*
and make sure my lips offer a continual praise
Contending for blessings that already belong to me
fighting a system man-made
Controlled by unseen negative forces
they're trying to stop the True Assembly from rising
Signs and wonders follow believers
religious demons are despising
The very foundation on which we stand
The Rock of all Ages
He's calling a people to die to self
because the rituals are overrated
The masses flee from the *Spirit of Truth*
because He's a *Spirit of Truth*
Lies are embraced in these evil days

SOLDIER STORIES: P.O.W.

we have to discern the trees and the fruit

There's a trendy saying "no filter"
but the *Set apart* scriptures can filter
The enemy doesn't want lives to truly change
subtle deception from the serial killer
Calling evil good and good evil
the propaganda is so deceitful
If you feed deception, it will grow
witness a generation of wounded people
With no sense of direction
reckless driving through intersections
No insurance coverage on the vehicles of life
while the *Body of Christ* has a hedge of protection

Persecution arises
demons use willing vessels to come against us
No weapon that is formed shall prosper
the *Shield of Faith* causes us to strike relentless
In season or out of season
angels war against demons
The *Word of ELOHIYM* is forever settled in heaven
there is hope for those breathing
I will stay upon my post
after the suffering, there's a reward
Extending a helping hand through poetry bars
standing as a *Prisoner of War*

Cornelius P. Thomas Jr.

THE POTTER'S WHEEL
Jeremiah 18:1-12, Isaiah 45:9

The winds are turbulent
the reactions are adverse
Demonic spirits are murdering
witness the pain of the curse
Whipped into patience and longsuffering
forced to leave a stain on each verse
Zion praises and testimonies I am uttering
ordained to be first
Because, we were positioned in last place
forced to be creative
Was running towards a dead end at a fast pace
constantly underrated

The curse has been reversed
the *Living Word* comes from my mouth
Living Waters flowing from my belly
urges me to shout the victory anyhow
Training in the valley
spinning on the *Potter's Wheel*
The opposite of spinning my wheels
the giant of fear has been killed!
Warring on this battlefield
is where you can find laborers that are effective
Delivered by the hand of YAH
by faith, we visualize different perspectives

The bigger picture
speaking life to withering expectations

SOLDIER STORIES: P.O.W.

I flee from impoverished mentalities and complacent
strategies, so there's separation
We witness casualties and worthless tragedies
YAH'S grace appreciated through meditation
I constantly think on YAH'S goodness
utilizing this treasure, dedication
Praying for direction
decreeing that I'm a lender, not a borrower
Praying for correction
many people talk "God," but they're not followers

There are rules of engagement
we do more giving than taking
The willing and obedient shall eat the good of the land
the *Blood of the Lamb* is against Satan
I pray to be used by *The Most High*
to hell with being seen by man
Man thrives off of ulterior motives
criticized whether I give up or stand
I possess a *Kingdom* mind frame so militant
now isn't the time for settling
The joy of YAH is our strength
we can't have joy without His presence

FROM THE PROCESS TO THE PROMISE

SOLDIER STORIES II
2 Timothy 2:1-4

I don't do this for the sport
I do this for the shortage
of those not reaching their full potential
In the rural or residential
areas
A citizen
but rejected by labels within America
I'm neck deep in this war
thus far, it's not emeritus
Is it that they're not hearing us?
Or trying to turn a deaf ear because they're feeling us?
Inwardly feeling dirty
restoration flow for the weariness
So many mistakes along the way
thankful for the power of forgiveness
Solely depending on the righteousness of the *Messiah*
His grace is sufficient
My *Source of Strength* when I'm weak
I have to remain faithful to His business
The ridicule has been my fuel
as I follow the lead of the *Inner Witness*
If you do a background check that is extensive
you'll find that I've been a warrior from birth
Attacked by this and survived that
what YAH has blessed, no man can curse
Even "I" must get out of dodge
to allow the flow of ELOHIYM'S increase
He's been far better than I can explain

Cornelius P. Thomas Jr.

so I worship with humility
In my members, there is another war
tugging and pushing, a continual toil
Temporary relief will welcome defeat
the lust of the flesh is the opposite of loyal
I wrestle within myself
but I have an *Ever-Present Help*
He changed my identity through the seal of *His* covenant
so the agenda of self
Is on the back burner, obsolete
The *Spirit of Truth* is persuasive
I can't blend in and follow the trends
I welcomed styles so innovative
I'm related like *"your fam"*
to the struggles in this land
Warring to obtain my inheritance and one single strand
of DNA gave me away
I AM of the blessed family
Forced to rise to the occasion
I yield for YAH to examine me
The metamorphosis is internal
urged to give my all for the cause
Carrying out marching orders from my *Colonel*
under grace, but bound to the law
Of the Spirit of Life in Jesus Christ
He ordered my steps so precise
It doesn't matter what it looks like
we are victorious in this fight

THE STRATEGY I
John 8:32, 36

Feels like I'm caught up in a wild goose chase
I search diligently for balance
because the just lives by faith
Calamities, adversities, infirmities, and afflictions
they all seem to arrive at my doorstep
around the same time
However, the enemy cannot overtake me
mankind continues to underrate me
EL YAHUAH is my *Hiding Place*
My *Rock* and *Ark of Safety*
Label me as a soldier in the trenches
ELOHIYM has revealed strategies unto me as a
Poetic and Kingdom Ambassador
My flesh flees from God-given visions
Today comes with a variety of options
new opportunities and undeniable hope
I constantly fumble with my own agenda
my life doesn't belong to me
Therefore, I had to surrender in order to be free
How can we sit by and watch a nation die?
I seek my *Savior* for wisdom, and ways to improvise
There is a remnant that is chasing after the beauty
of YAH, they desire change
We have to apply our focus to allowing YAH to
transform us that we can effectively teach the
generations to come
Elevate mental states to rise above the slums
we can eat at the royal table

Cornelius P. Thomas Jr.

Why settle for the crumbs?
Poor mentalities, poverty-stricken impulsive decisions
financial illiteracy, the hand outs
The true ELOHIYM is *Alpha and Omega*
Today, I can laugh in the face of reality
The threats of trouble will fade away
when the *Spirit of Truth* comes on the scene
The masses are deceived by *"get rich quick"* schemes
million dollar dreams and mediocre thinking
Nevertheless, the Saints should not fail to sow
into YAH'S Kingdom
To whom much is given, much is required
inwardly, I aspire
to give my all for the replenishing of the hungry souls
Jesus can fill the voids of those who have been wounded
He has laborers in the vineyard and soldiers
in His mighty army
We are called to plant, water, and cultivate
the potential seeds
ELOHIYM himself gives the increase
If you are seeking spiritual growth
human reasoning must cease
Revelation knowledge overthrows my thought pattern
I can't hold the truth in
The illumination from the *Ruach Elohiym*
strategic plans from my pen

SOLDIER STORIES: P.O.W.

THE STRATEGY II
Jeremiah 4, 17:4

Many people view "God" only through the lenses of the
geographical location of a church building
However, the "True Assembly" will experience
the glory of YAH
…a great theophany
A universal revival is at hand
Following the leadership of the *Holy Spirit*
is an everyday journey
The choice is yours
Will you surrender and embrace the denial of self to
apprehend the King of kings?
The battle is underway, deception is all around
We have to stay connected to our *Lifeline*
Jesus has given us the power to procreate
as the new breed of Abraham's seed
There is power in prayer
results are found in the Messiah's name
Without faith, it is impossible to please Him
FAITH: *For All I Trust Him*
He will overthrow the ways of the trouble maker
The *True and Living* ELOHIYM will expose
the devil's representatives
I will not be bound by man's expectation of me
and fail to please Father YAH
Any day, I would rather be used by Him
than to be seen by men
We are more than conquerors through *Him* that loved us
In yesteryear, I was least likely to succeed

Cornelius P. Thomas Jr.

The *Spirit of YAH* is my *Leader*
therefore, I was given grace to proceed
I trust Him to weed out the real from the pretenders
The name *"Israel" (Yisra'el)* was given to Jacob
ELOHIYM'S chosen
Today, the twelve tribes of Israel still thrives
However, deception has filled the land
YAH'S *Elect* has been mocked and even they
have fallen for the lies
The denial of self is necessary
vain glory is obsolete
I am greedy for more of ELOHIYM'S presence
The power, authority, and accuracy of the *Ruach* is
tugging on the hearts of this great nation…
…to form a spiritual and mental alliance
we must rise above the worldly system's design
YAH is establishing a divine order
and revealing Kingdom principles
Impure motives, hidden agendas, evil intentions and
carnal minds have to cease
*Why is it that there is so much oppression, bondage, and
division in the land of the free?*
*Or should I say among those who were supposed to line
up with precepts of The Most High*
We overlook the "real enemy"
but find fault in one another
Judah is dwelling in lands of captivity
But, the *Spirit of Truth* isn't bound
We must exercise <u>2nd Chronicles 7:14</u>
The favor of YAH is profound!

THE STRATEGY III
1 Peter 2:9

In this day, we cannot afford to take anything for granted
The ELOHIYM of Abraham, Isaac, and Jacob
is Sovereign
No sinful flesh can glory in His presence
we dwell under an open heaven
YAH has stretched forth His hands
looking for a people who thirst for *Living Waters*
We must put away all hidden agendas
we must repent and turn wholly unto the
Living ELOHIYM
He has cleansed and purged us from all unrighteousness
Those who worship the Father
must worship Him in *Spirit and truth*
In this army, we have to forsake division and any other
problems that we may have with a brother or sister
We should embrace the comradery, loyalty, and unity
expressed by the natural armed forces
This *Holy Nation* will not operate like *"Lady Liberty"*
the hypocrite
We have to possess the knowledge and awareness of
our rights as *Recipients of the Covenant*
The Messiah fulfilled the law and through Him,
we possess a better covenant
We can only keep the commandments, as we yield unto
the Holy *Spirit of YAH*
We have to become a reflection of the Light which flows
from the *"Resurrected One"*
The *Eternal pages of Life* cannot lie

Cornelius P. Thomas Jr.

Yet, we must remain in right standing
with this *Living Word*
The *Master* will not change *His* Word or ways for man
therefore, we have to jump on His bandwagon
The Messiah has redeemed us from the curse of the law
the debt and threat of sin
The *Body of Believers* shall stand, seeing that now
circumcision of the heart is required
Regardless of vain opinions, the message of ELOHIYM
is one of love to all who will embrace Him
And one of terror and great wrath to those who oppose
His supernatural invitation
Whether one is classified as "Jew" or "Gentile"
The book of *Ephesians,* the second chapter declares that
the two became "One new man" reconciled to Father
YAH in *One Body,* The Messiah being the *Head*
He said that we must HEAR WHAT THE SPIRIT
is saying to the *Church*
We have to embrace our pilgrimage and assignments
Individually, as well as collectively
ELOHIYM has redeemed us with a proof of purchase
In this world, we are treated as rejects and outcasts
greater is *He* that is in me than he that is in the world
We are called to stand strong
we have been seated in heavenly places
Our *Avenger* isn't sleep
He will have the last laugh!

THE STRATEGY IV
Ecclesiastes 7:5, 1 Peter 2:9

The order and command to convert nations have
already been ordained, plotted, and finished
before the foundations of the world
We have been labeled as
Replenishers of a Desolate Land
No choice but to take a stand
We have been given a mandate to accept life, and speak
life, as we represent *Life* in this dying world
We have to acknowledge the power of thoughts
the battles take place in the mind
If Satan can poison our minds
then he will dilute our beliefs
If he can distract our focus
then he can silence our confessions
However, we have a solid foundation
The *ROCK* on which this mighty nation stands
Jesus Christ
The phrase *"Lyrical"* is simply the *Word of* ELOHIYM
composed in a poetic design, which exposes the
mysteries of the *Spirit*, the testimonies, phases, and
stages of myself, and those who favor the righteous
cause, whom YAH has called out of darkness
into His marvelous light
Those who were least likely to succeed,
or hidden and abused among the thieves
now called to lead quiet and peaceable lives
However, we pledge our allegiance to the *King of Kings*
and embrace Kingdom principles

Cornelius P. Thomas Jr.

We will not bow in reverence to this whore's system
which has perverted relationship found through salvation
and promoted religion as a means of financial gain
and identity theft
The phrase *"Giant"* describes how we, as a nation
can trample over all of the giants of oppression,
depression, sickness, lack, sin, and so on
I AM a giant killer, trained to effectively use my weapon
The WORD of ELOHIYM
The *Word* will stand tall, as all other methods,
philosophies and doctrines crumble
"Lyrical Giant" this is a movement!
We must commit to re-educating ourselves
first and foremost spiritually, because all kinds of
deceptive spirits and doctrines have been loosed!
The *Elect* has been deceived and led astray
Now, we need to properly become equipped for battle
There is no mercy in war!
The devil has never been merciful with mankind
therefore, we must strike relentless
ELOHIYM has provided instructions and armor
we must study the rules of engagement
The art and secrets to war
I take this war seriously!
We have warring angels dispatched on our behalf
we have to become good stewards over all
that has been committed unto us
Integrity and faithfulness is what will carry us through
We must educate our kids on the issues of peer pressure,
sin, and the overall reality of life in general
This is no time to be timid or pretend

the devil manipulate the kids through a need
to be accepted
Let them know that ELOHIYM has already accepted
them through the finished work of Christ
We can't fully function, unless we remain unified
Let us embrace the *"we are a team"* or bond expressed
by our natural law enforcement
Let us embrace healthy lifestyles
after all, we have *Resurrection Power*
operating on the inside of us
We have to exercise discipline
our bodies are the sacred temples
We can't proclaim YAH to be a *Healer* and in the same
breath, walk around defeated in our bodies
Let us take on the *"our nation is the strongest"* attitude
of the United States
Most of all let us follow the example of our ancestors
and forefathers, the heroes of faith (before the idolatry)
These examples are found in our rulebook
the manuscript
Our **(B)** *asic* **(I)** *nstructions* **(B)** *efore* **(L)** *eaving* **(E)** *arth*
Let us take honor in what the *Ancient of Days*
and His Son, our *Savior, the Great High Priest*
has made possible for us
We have to always acknowledge our *Mentor, Teacher,*
Comforter, our Strength, the Holy Spirit
Let us present our bodies as living sacrifices
this world is not our home
However, we will leave our marks
as a testimony against it
Let us acknowledge the revelation and the suffering

Cornelius P. Thomas Jr.

of our *Messiah* whom they hung on the tree
Through His *Eternal Sacrifice,* we obtain the promises,
liberty, and favor poured out upon the *Body*
Let us press on to greatness!

THE STRATEGY V
Matthew 24:13

The devil cannot overthrow the operation of the Spirit
if our minds are transformed and renewed
Satan can't infiltrate the power of mind strength
Yet, when we open our mouths and begin to speak
then demonic spirits have a right to cheat
This means that our words have to line up with the *Word*
Our *Defense*
In the light of YAH'S countenance
imperfections are exposed
However, we must strive for perfection
sin has caused love to wax cold
The believers must display compassion and affection
We have to commit to performing
at a standard of excellence
Responsibility, reliability, accountability, dependability
We all have the "ability" to let the *Light of Christ*
shine through our lives
Love has to be seen through our actions
life provides opportunities and purposes to fulfill
Action eliminates acting
it always speaks louder than words
*What good is quoting scriptures, if we don't operate in
the power and authority of the Holy Spirit of YAH?*
This letter is not for finger pointing
the messengers are the first to get cut with
the *Sword of The Most High*
Souls are lost and confused
feeling like they constantly have to lose

Cornelius P. Thomas Jr.

Jesus can set the captives free
we have to study to show ourselves approved
Strange doctrines and compromising spirits
work together to bring minds into captivity
Nevertheless, *Resurrection Power* overthrows
death and darkness
It is imperative that we remain teachable, and never let
the wisdom of men replace the *Spirit* who knows all
Greatness is at the finish line!
We must endure hardness as good soldiers
the war is for souls!
Every day, at all times, we have a battle to fight
every time we do good, evil is present
the road gets lonely
Your natural eyes and ears will attempt to deceive you
however, quitting is not an option
Many of our neighbors are held captive
under the influence of the enemy
The bondage of sin provides a category for humans
called *"The Walking Dead"*
There is no doubt in my mind that situations can
and will turn around!
We are YAH'S hands, feet, and mouthpieces in the earth
nevertheless, we have to stay out of *His* way
The greater works of redemption are at hand
we've been chosen to become walking, living epistles
Portable tabernacles
Communication rules the nation
information is limited
Revelation will be documented
on the tree, Yahusha has finished it

SOLDIER STORIES: P.O.W.

What did the Savior finish?
Anything that we may encounter
on this uncertain journey
The *Blood of the Lamb* has redeemed us
from the hands of the enemy
Many still don't know
the people perish for a lack of knowledge
This is why we, as a whole, can't mature and grow
Spiritual gifts, talents, and callings are woven
into your authentic purpose
We must follow the plan that has already been laid out
and conduct ourselves as true disciples
There is hope for the lost souls that seek shelter
this world is not our home
However, they are watching to see
if the *True Assembly* will stand strong

Cornelius P. Thomas Jr.

IN ALL THY WAYS
Proverbs 3:3-6

My information is limited
I don't suggest that you copy me
I wait on instructions from the Holy Spirit
without Him, I'll operate sloppily
The hypocrisy can easily be seen
if I depend on my own ability
The anointing can destroy the yokes of bondage
it causes me to speak with liberty
Effectively
The *Messiah* can set men free!
I seek Him to constantly make me over
and help me flee from envy
Strife, pride, and self-righteousness
the broad path welcomes destruction
If I sow to my flesh
from my flesh, I'll reap corruption
Since my understanding is finite
I pray to discern the prophetic
The commandments are in my heart embedded
perfect love is the eternal message
For being blessed, I won't be apologetic
hate to sound harsh
Life will not wait on me to get it together
therefore, I pray to be set apart
Effectively dodging fiery darts
learning from the mistakes
To YAH, I commit and submit my way
He has prepared the path that I'll take

SOLDIER STORIES: P.O.W.

forsaking my own thoughts and ways
Had to die to self to take a stand
A slave to righteousness who seeks favor
and understanding in the sight of ELOHIYM and man

Cornelius P. Thomas Jr.

WARFARE IN THE HEAT OF THE DAY
Joshua 10:8-14

The situation doesn't line up with the revelation
Nevertheless, the anointing is being stirred
gifts deposited from the world's foundation
In an obscure, dry desert place
this is where many radical believers are planted to grow
"His story" has ordained destiny
Jesus Christ is the *Head of the Body*
Daily, I die for Him to live within
I thank the Father for my enemies
in this season of persecution
This is a strategic phase that I must go through
before I get promoted to the next phase of life
Praising YAHUAH in advance for divine connections
solid kinsmen that will complete me
and not compete against me
I duck and dodge fiery darts
We will never win if we fight this war with feelings
Instead, I keep my faith in *The Most High* and a pen
handy to hear what the *Spirit* is saying to the Church
The *Blood of the Lamb* is against everything
that isn't like Him!
What matter of circumstance can stand?
...when a faith-filled soldier is speaking in the land?
Marching in the heat of the sun
even though the battle has been won
There are still rules of engagement that we must follow

In the event that I enter in among a pit of snakes,

SOLDIER STORIES: P.O.W.

I will be clothed with the Armor of ELOHIYM
prepared to do battle with the *Sword of the Spirit*
The weapons of our warfare are not carnal
and the invitations are not formal
but, rather deceptive
Praise, worship, and my daily confessions
keep me focused
Focused on overthrowing limitations and going into the
enemy's camp to get all that he has stolen from me
The power is in prayer
In the name of Yahusha, all of the powers of darkness
are driven backwards
YAHUAH trains, shapes, and molds His soldiers
We're often confronted by adversaries
and tried by adversity
Shaped and molded to stand tall in the *Spirit*
the truth will always come with controversy

Blessings are predestined
prophecies were foretold
We have to go through it to get to it
Weapons have been drawn against me to do battle
but they will not prosper
We must constantly put the devil in remembrance
of the eternal defeat that took place at Calvary
The art of war is to stand when circumstances suggest
failure, and surroundings are filled with negativity
I refuse to bow to these idols
I possess the strength and resilience of a Giant Killer
I call upon the ELOHIYM of war to go before me
the victory is found in my confession!

Cornelius P. Thomas Jr.

The power and authority that we walk in is delegated
I follow the instructions, as the Holy Spirit leads
The situation doesn't line up with the revelation
the critics, naysayers, and spectators
will witness the manifestations
In the heat of the day we need a fan
but not to sit back and be cool
Against all odds, YAH will open doors
we have to be conditioned to walk through

BY THE HAND OF YAH
Exodus 3:1-10

Exodus
a movement of the people
Delivered by the *hand of YAH*
make way for this poetic sequel
Many generations after
we flip the pages to new chapters
War cries to the world
for His name's sake, we've been captured

Delivered by the *hand of YAH*
time after time
He is *Faithful* who has promised us
broken hearts repent at this rhyme
The *Bridegroom* mourns for *His Bride*
heavenly revelations and exposed mysteries
ELOHIYM is not the author of confusion
yet the *Church* has embraced captivity
Through tradition, religion, division
and mental segregation
Instead of relationships that are strengthened
through faithful dedication

YAH is married to the backslider
ready to counsel and nurture
He that hates his brother is bound by a spirit of murder
The *Good News* has to spread and go further
Deep into the hearts of men
down within secret chambers

Cornelius P. Thomas Jr.

I utter the praises of a stranger
protected by angels from danger
Delivered by the *hand of YAH*
as Bible prophecy sets the stage for *Armageddon*
Please embrace this war cry
in these seasons of testing

Exodus
we can't be scared to trust
In the *True and Living* ELOHIYM
who has always been there for us
The *Father* sacrificed *His Son*
for our reconciliation
Our *Refuge* in the *Beginning of Sorrows*
He will be a *Shield* for those in the *Great Tribulation*
Holy *Spirit* is our liberation
in the midst of countless situations
The *Great High Priest* acts as a lawyer
He pled a countless list of cases
before the *accuser of the brethren*
YAH and His angels are Judge and jury
His clients are sealed unto the day of redemption
demonic spirits may try to lure me
but they don't have any dominion

Delivered by the *hand of YAH*
I'm determined to stand on the *Word*
because the naked *Truth* will overthrow a dressed up lie
The Holy Prophets are killed
on this foreign battlefield
It's an honor and privilege to represent YAH

SOLDIER STORIES: P.O.W.

He is our *Source* and our *Shield*

They know not what they do
as we praise Him in advance for our breakthroughs
We have to use our faith to
forgive the blind and hateful
Jesus is *faithful*
The *Groom* mourns for the *Church*
faithful are the wounds of a *Friend*
We all know that love hurts
Or should I say the Truth hurts?
Whether Truth or Love
He is our Life
The name of ADONAI is a *Strong Tower*
we have access through the risen Christ

Cornelius P. Thomas Jr.

ONE LIFE AT A TIME
1 Corinth 3:7-11

In order to enjoy great victory
we have to conquer great conflict
Saved by grace through faith
the roads of uncertainty are constant
Serving YAH will pay off
these words will pay off
His grace welcomes trouble
the struggle never takes a day off
We have to keep praying and pressing
constantly seek Him for wisdom and direction
Have to look beyond what our eyes can see
and guide our affairs with discretion
With different spirits, minds are wrestling
I speak life over dead situations
Many dreams were murdered by circumstance
this diluted determination
These words that I speak
uniquely hides behind Jesus name
Soldier stories filled with His goodness
favor, mercy, and eternal gain
Hardships and heartaches
can't finish strong if you start fake
Putting confidence in man
will only lead to heartbreaks
Satan will only use what is familiar
from faces to tactics
Seems like it's easier to hate
As we shake these issues and unwanted baggage

SOLDIER STORIES: P.O.W.

I asked YAH to let me become the change
that I desire to see in others
One life at a time
we'll find YAH'S mercy uncovered

Cornelius P. Thomas Jr.

NOTHING IS IMPOSSIBLE FOR GOD
Genesis 18:14, Jeremiah 32:27
Matthew 19:26, Luke 1:37

There's nothing impossible for God
at times, we can't see when we're going through
I've been blessed with another perspective
seated in heavenly places with a better view
As I look down on circumstances
the storm doesn't define who *I AM*
Chosen and trained as a young warrior
to the very end expected to stand
With my hands lifted up
and my mouth filled with praise
I am nothing without Him
Want God to get the glory in all of my days
As I get attacked, can't sit complacent
there are rules of engagement
The battles have been won, but we have to fight
can't run from the conflict, we have to face it

There's nothing impossible for God
at times, we can't see when we're going through
The enemy will try to suppress your praise
we speak to mountains for them to move
They may not move when you first speak it
embrace boldness and believe it
The *Word of God* shall stand
these trials are strategic
Find me in a place of submission
spectators can't figure my worship

SOLDIER STORIES: P.O.W.

They're waiting to see if God will rescue me
watch me rise through the hardships
Had to leave that place of puppy love courtship
and move to a deeper level of intimacy
Holy *Spirit* has promised to flood the *Church*
Christ reigns infinitely
The devil has stolen some of my possessions
he's really after my joy
I can see the ambush, the trickery
the threats and decoys

I will not be moved!
There's nothing impossible for God
standing against all odds
The natural realm is full of facades
Already have a word in my mouth by the time
that the heat comes to my front door
Headed to a new level in Christ
a place that I've never witnessed before
Real faith, He can't ignore
every time my feet hit the floor
The mission is to run my assignment
and testify that He lives, as I soar

Cornelius P. Thomas Jr.

BLESS THE LORD AT ALL TIMES
Psalms 34

My heart is reprovable
because the *Word of God* is immutable
I speak to the mountains by faith
I know that the mountains are movable
The opposing armies are listening
as I speak life into the atmosphere
They want me to give up and quit
however I curse the bondage of fear
I will obtain everything
that has been ordained for me to have
Documenting through the pain
I still have joy on this path
The world didn't give it to me
no devil can take it away
I don't have to take "no" for an answer
these battles are give and take
Gaining wisdom from past mistakes
called to stand, my life was predestined
It doesn't always feel good when you have to own up
to your faults and learn your lesson
Praise is my secret weapon
it's a sacrifice to keep praise on my lips
Jesus was obedient all the way to the cross
His example allows me to get a grip
This is why my expectations won't slip
and allow me to get in unbelief
The *Truth* has exposed the thief
reparations belong to me!

SOLDIER STORIES: P.O.W.

Satan hasn't gotten away with anything
I constantly cry out to my King
to avenge me of my adversary
while I keep a song in my heart to sing
From sunrise to sunset
we have a mandate to bless God
He can turn situations around in an instance
even though we're against all odds
I summon the *God of War*
bold, because I possess a Lion's heart
The *Lion from Judah's tribe* dwells inside
He has commissioned me to play my part
He has reconciled us unto the Father
when He conquered death, hell, and the grave
Because He's *Alpha and Omega*
I can conquer any obstacle that's in my way
The *Living Word* is within me
the *Living Word* is not bound
The *Word* is connected to my living faith
all things are mine right now!
I will bless the Lord at all times
His praise shall continually be in my mouth
despite how it looks at this present moment
Jesus won the championship bout

Cornelius P. Thomas Jr.

THE SNIPER
Judges 6:12

As a sniper, I launch grenades
to free minds from captivity
Reversing the attacks with a counter-attack
to spoil demonic activity
Healing flows from the rhymes
YAH has planted fruitful vines
The roots are soaking in *Living Waters*
my purpose defined
Many won't be able to comprehend it
there's a remnant with faith in attendance
Moving mountains while counting
every second and minute
Inside of the last hours
our time has to be effectively utilized
Without the cross, there's no crown
every day, we have to be crucified
A fleshly death
success comes with jealousy and envy
War has risen against me
been through too much to let it offend me!
The battles belong to YAH
the victory is ours
Victory means nothing without the lesson
the lessons contain the true power
The *Spirit of Truth* dwells on the inside
with the joy of YAH, I am inspired
Have to keep in mind through strenuous tests
that gold is tried by the fire

SOLDIER STORIES: P.O.W.

Words of pain, words of flame
the words of redemption
Words of faith that reflect hope and divine intervention
Everyone will pay what they owe
there will be no extensions
I hunger and thirst after righteousness
longing for deeper dimensions
There are poisonous reptiles in the trenches
many are struggling to find true value
Undefiled love versus perverted lust
the believers are engaged in real battles
Promotion comes neither from the east or west
ELOHIYM crowns men with the chance
For the light to shine in troubled times
either fall short or advance
This movement is not a trend
constantly laboring, because it's a brand
Branded by the *Blood of the Lamb*
change is in high demand
Among those who are in love with YAH
I am greedy for more of YAH'S presence
As a sniper, I launch grenades
until He returns me to my essence
Trials and tribulations
so many sticky situations
I'm confident, because my *Redeemer* lives
I represent liberation
This war is for souls
the imposters will be exposed
Through the discernment of spirits
the *Anointing* causes us to properly grow

Cornelius P. Thomas Jr.

EFFECTIVE IMMEDIATELY
2 Peter 1:4-8

Don't mistake me for a simple foot soldier
that doesn't have the ability to think clearly
I trust EL SHADDAI for all things
He restores my soul when I get weary
We must effectively follow orders
if we plan to effectively lead
The Covenant is greater than material possessions
obedience cultivates the good seed
Once a man isn't afraid to die
he never has to worry about being defeated
The devil loves to sell wolf tickets
in a land where souls are depleted
As I undergo construction
I realize that the *Living Word* can't be compromised
So I set my affections on things above
the truth will prevail and confront the lies
Liabilities can't be utilized
we capitalize off of assets
The infirmities of the weak are carried by the strong
love is underneath the war fabrics
We will continue to shout the victory
at times, the war can get strenuous
The *Elect* has angels on assignment
YAH inhabits praises that are continuous
If a man hasn't discovered something that he's willing
to die for, then he isn't fit to live
I've exchanged my faith for greater faith
my life, I have to yield and give

SOLDIER STORIES: P.O.W.

Holy *Spirit* is my *Leader*
He's my *Mentor* and *Promoter*
I'm part of a tribe of soldiers
who refuse to roll over
Can't go to war without spoils
lost souls are on the line
Precious in the sight of YAH
the reason why I document throughout my lifetime
Yahusha is my *Lifeline*
there's a constant death for me
Until I breathe the last breath in me
called to expose the depth of me
The *Ruach ELOHIYM* is *He*
He pours the strategies unto paper
A journey of a million miles is vain
without the love of the *Promise Maker*
My faith is my source of strength
ELOHIYM is my *Source*, the suspense
of this action packed thriller called *"life"*
many times, doesn't make sense
YAH will judge Babylon
He'll arise and scatter his enemies
The media's job is to suppress our true identities
camouflaged like they possess righteous tendencies
These war rhymes are essential, seeing that many are
positioned in a valley experience
Discipline is required, don't become a lab rat
in the government's experiment
The system is controlled by Satan
but the Father has the final say
Yahusha, the *Eternal Sacrifice* to an abundant life

Cornelius P. Thomas Jr.

don't allow these demons to infiltrate
The sacred components of your mental
or the secret chambers of your heart
The *Children of the Light* are sealed unto the day
of redemption, set apart

SOLDIER STORIES: P.O.W.

THE EXECUTION OF MARCHING ORDERS
James 2:17-18

A proposal of peace unaccompanied
by a sworn covenant indicates a plot
We have to pray and watch the signs
because *spirits of deception* will not stop
When I get free from individual conflict
my brother may be subdued in personal battles
Divide and conquer are the enemy's tactics
so productive energy is what we channel
With the intent to unify
kingdoms that are divided will welcome failure
We were not given the spirit of fear
come and pick the mind of a storyteller
He who exercises no forethought
but takes his enemy for granted
Will be captured by the opposition
isolated and left stranded
The *Messiah* has promised to never leave
or forsake any of His troops
We can easily step out of His will
have to be prepared to bounce back and regroup
There's a certain road to victory
the travelers have to submit to spiritual discipline
Consistent prayers and supplications
will overcome frustration, relentless men
Will proceed to cover more grounds
we must work while it's called *Today*
Have to keep in mind that souls are on the line
our faith is constantly on display

Cornelius P. Thomas Jr.

If the grounds are accessible
either side can advance
The good or the evil
don't be soon shaken by the circumstance
Faith becomes our eyes to secure our supplies
our God will provide
I exalt Him as EL SHADDAI
The armies of the enemy are always prepared
we have to stand guard
The *Watchmen* give themselves to intercession
knowing that there's healing in place for battle scars
The *General* who advances
without coveting fame
Instead, he continues to die daily
in order to exalt the *Savior's* name
In the face of strenuous opposition
he can retreat without fearing disgrace
He or she has a total dependency on God
the name of YAH is their hiding place
That particular *Under-Shepherd* is the jewel of the
Kingdom, because he honors a greater authority
He or she doesn't fear persecution
as they feed their flocks, labeled as royalty
The *General* exercises loyalty
among decorated officers and foot soldiers
In the event of utter destruction
in the *Resting Place*, we can remain sober
Documentation from a Kingdom Ambassador
in training to follow the marching orders
We overcome by our testimonies and the Blood of the
Lamb approved by the Father

AMEN
Revelation 3:14

He is the *One* to seal the deal
the *Amen*
I've been sealed to the day of redemption
born again to win
Blessed with a new day
but called to stick to the same sayings
If life is a game
then we must stick to the game plan
Fascinated with being captivated
by the *Spirit of Truth*
Faith is activated, character assassinated
forced to bounce back and regroup
Mocked due to misfortune
true warriors are defined by adversity
The grace to endure comes from YAH
my attempts to claim fame unworthily
Will never be detected
been rejected since day one
If there are no open doors for me
then I trust ELOHIYM to create some
To whom much is given
much is required
Gold is tried in the fire
have to keep on the proper attire
Warfare exists on a daily basis
the devil is a liar
Deceived by smiles on familiar faces
on a mission to go higher

Cornelius P. Thomas Jr.

The *Messiah*
The *Amen*
is at the end of a life span
He's also the *Beginning of Procreation*
The *Creator* of every nation and land
I utter *"so be it"*
all that I'm destined to be
I curse premature death at the root
Covenant blessings belong to me
I want all that has been promised
especially the promises that I haven't possessed yet
My destiny is to leave a legacy
refuse to accept the death threat
I keep praying and crying out
until what I see is accessible
Until I reach the *Amen* of the story
defeat is unacceptable
There are more chapters ahead
available for the *Spirit of Truth* to use me
A partaker and recipient of great miracles
called to remain faithful to the duty
Amen.

Scripture References

Original King James Version 1611 Apocrypha included

Holy Bible

The Scriptures (Institute for Scripture Research)

www.ingramcontent.com/pod-product-compliance
Lightning Source LLC
Chambersburg PA
CBHW050648160426
43194CB00010B/1854